THE NEW
BIBLE JUMBLE

THE NEW
BIBLE JUMBLE

A Book of Unscrambled Words

John Troy McQueen

authorHOUSE®

AuthorHouse™ LLC
1663 Liberty Drive
Bloomington, IN 47403
www.authorhouse.com
Phone: 1-800-839-8640

Published by AuthorHouse   09/26/2013

ISBN: 978-1-4918-2097-1 (sc)
ISBN: 978-1-4918-2096-4 (e)

INTRODUCTION

The New Bible Jumble is a book of words to unscramble, in order to form words to find in a hidden puzzle. It is similar to the "Jumble Words" found in most daily newspaper.

All the underlined letters are the ones to help the reader find a new word. Only four words are included in each puzzle. The first two words have five letters and the second two words have six letters. The numbers on the line tells how many letters are found in the word for the clue. A clue is given for each puzzle.

All the words in the puzzle are found in a Bible Dictionary. The answers to the unscrambled words and clues we found in the back of the book.

The book is written to enrich the reader's Bible knowledge. This will be an excellent book for: passing the time while traveling on an airplane, train, bus, subway, trolley, a ship, or automobile. Young people and adults could make use of this book for activities; such as, for Sunday School, Vacation Bible School, Christian Schools and more.

L I O S P

T O S O L

H E L S I D

D I N K Y E

The Sabbath is a day of rest. Remember it and keep . . .

——————— ———————
   (2)   (4)

I̲ L̲ T H G

T N A P L̲

L L I̲ P W̲ O̲

D N R A G̲ E

The Prophet Isaiah said he saw the Lord in the year King Uzziah died. The question was asked, "Who Shall I Send?" Isaiah said . . .

"_____ _____ _____"
  (1)   (4)   (2)

H T A I F

E D U J G

R P I A S E

M B U N R E

We should love the sinner, but . . .

" _____ _____ _____ "
   (4)   (1)   (3)

N G A L E

L N A G O

N V I I G R

T S E L T E

"For God so loved the world that He gave His only
begotten son, that whosoever believeth on Him should
have eternal life."

_____ _____ _____
(3)   (2)   (4)

E S B R O

A S T Y E

G R E N O I

C U S I S D

Parents should start early in teaching their children to stay away from worldly pleasures.

_____ (3)   _____ (2)   _____ (2)   _____ (5)

T R I B H

S E F L A

P E E L D Y

R U L B A I

The Israelites ate manna in the wilderness. This is similar
today to . . .

_____   _____
(3)   (5)

NHT<u>O</u><u>M</u>

T<u>E</u>PAR

NADLA<u>S</u>

OUEM<u>S</u>

To lead the Israelites he had to have a character that was Christlike.

_____

(5)

H E W T A

A N T A S

A R T R Y M

I T N A Y V

Jonah went to another city trying to hide from God.

_____   _____   _____
    (2)   (3)   (4)

R A E H T

A V N L E

A T H D E

N O L Y O C

To become this he must have "an honest report, wisdom and full of the Holy Ghost."

_____ _____

(1)   (6)

H <u>A</u> E <u>S</u> L

<u>O</u> U <u>G</u> D R

<u>N</u> T C E <u>I</u> S

<u>N</u> <u>G</u> I L <u>S</u> E

When the Israelites were in Babylon, they began to . . .

_____ _____ _____
  (4)   (1)   (4)

BATEL

UNOYG

NETODR

TSAMRE

A person willing to die for his belief.

_____   _____
(1)   (6)

R I P̲ D E̲

V E L̲ O̲ I

W A̲ Y̲ L R E̲

T A O S P̲ M̲

What Ruth said to Naomi, when they went back to
Bethlehem . . .

_____ _____
  (2)   (6)

A L S M E

D R C A E

T T E C L A

D L W M E I

When Lazarus was raised from the dead is an example of . . .

_____ _____
(1)   (7)

A L <u>L</u> H S

<u>E</u> E <u>R</u> G N

K A <u>A</u> H M T E

R G <u>E</u> E E <u>D</u>

Joshua was a strong . . .

———

(6)

H T G O S

H E N O R

N E A F M I

E E E L F C

What Jesus told His Apostles if they followed Him, what
He would make them . . .

| (1) | (6) | (2) | (3) |

K I C R B

L A I S N

D A F G Y L

P I R D S E

All the other surrounding countries had one. The people went to Samuel. He told them to choose . . .

_____   _____
(1)   (4)

N N A A M

C K O F L

W S R D O

R E V Q I U

Gideon was a mighty . . .

_____ _____ _____
(3)   (2)   (5)

K O R B̲ O

T̲ E O̲ N̲ A

L B A M Y̲ C

G̲ P S̲ N̲ R I̲

How Stephen was killed . . .

—————— ——————
(2)   (7)

A I U Q L

D D D E A

M M L A B E

N N A T O I

After the walls were destroyed, Nehemiah and the people had a . . .

_____ _____ _____
(4)   (2)   (5)

H A C I N

C E R A G

D R G A N E

T A S E C L

David was a man after God's own . . .

———

(5)

G L <u>A</u> N E

T <u>N</u> H <u>I</u> G

<u>R</u> <u>I</u> <u>V</u> H E S

L D P E E <u>G</u>

Mary, the mother of Jesus, was . . .

_____ (1)   _____ (6)

HA<u>S</u>GN

H<u>T</u><u>N</u>G<u>I</u>

<u>P</u>PRO<u>C</u>E

RRMA<u>O</u>Y

John's gospel was not . . .

———

(8)

E <u>M</u> R <u>Y</u> C

R <u>A</u> <u>S</u> B <u>S</u>

S <u>N</u> N O <u>I</u> <u>O</u>

P <u>I</u> <u>R</u> S T I

Paul was the first . . .

——————
(10)

U T M O H

N G R A E

S A T M R E

T N E A R P

James warned that we should be in control of our . . .

(7)

O S E R W

R O W P E

A N L E H D

E W L A H T

Be not deceived, God is not mocked. We will . . .

" _____ _____ _____ _____ "
   (4)   (4)   (2)   (3)

T R O F S

U I T R F

O N A T O I

S T G A I N

This took place on the mountain, after Jesus fasted for forty days.

(14)

R <u>O</u> W <u>N</u> <u>C</u>

<u>O</u> <u>R</u> N <u>S</u> E

<u>A</u> <u>G</u> R I L C

<u>H</u> E <u>S</u> <u>U</u> B L

Jesus paid it all. He . . .

_____ _____ _____ _____

(4)　　　　(2)　　　　(1)　　　　(5)

<u>A</u> <u>V</u> E H <u>S</u>

<u>O</u> O N N <u>I</u>

<u>A</u> <u>N</u> R E U T

S E <u>T</u> <u>L</u> O C

It is free. God wants us to be saved. We must believe that God raised Jesus from the dead.

----

(9)

E T N S T

H C O R P

N G E U T O

A E L W H T

The first five books of the Bible are called the . . .

(10)

B̲ R̲ U̲ H S̲

G̲ H̲ I T L

R D U̲ B̲ N̲ E

R E W̲ N̲ I̲ T

God spoke to Moses at a . . .

_____ _____
(7)   (4)

God is the supreme authority. He is Creator and Ruler of the universe. He is everywhere.

(9)

T A W̲ H̲ C

D̲ E E̲ W̲ G

L L C S̲ R̲ O

O D R̲ N P A̲

In the beginning . . .

_____ _____ _____
(3)   (3)   (4)

E A R S P

N G A L E

R I P C T S

S L A I T R

Joseph and Mary were Jesus . . .

———————

(7)

G H I̲ T N̲

N N A̲ A̲ M̲

R E̲ N̲ I S G̲

I I T S R̲ P

There were no room in the Inn. So Jesus was born . . .

———— (2)   ———— (1)   ———— (6)

O P R E W

H N I T G

S N E D M O

S T E L A C

He left home and spent all of his money in worldly pleasures.

_____ _____ _____
(3)   (8)   (3)

R E W <u>P</u> <u>O</u>

R E S <u>P</u> <u>S</u>

T L A <u>H</u> W E

P M <u>E</u> <u>E</u> <u>T</u> L

Deborah was a . . .

———

(10)

N E I S W̲

E A̲ W̲ T̲ S

R̲ T̲ L A S I̲

G I N̲ L E̲ O̲

Jesus performed His first miracle at a wedding by turning . . .

_____ _____ _____
(5) (4) (4)

O T̲ H̲ O B̲

I N H̲ G̲ T̲

N E R̲ S H I̲

R̲ T E S S I̲

Jacob stole his twin brother's . . .

———

(10)

L A I N P

R I P D E

E E S S V L

L L I O W W

John The Baptist baptized Jesus. He preached in the . . .

———————

(10)

N T L <u>A</u> <u>P</u>

<u>R</u> I <u>B</u> T E

H E<u>R</u> C <u>A</u> R

I M N A A <u>L</u>

The Good Samaritan was an earthly story, with a Heavenly meaning called a . . .

---

(7)

O O R B K

N S G W I

H A D W S O

R E T Y S U

Ezekiel preached to a valley of . . .

_____ _____
    (3)   (5)

L̲ E̲ F B A

S̲ S̲ E P R

D̲ M E̲ A I D

A S K T B̲ E

The Beatitudes begin with . . .

---

(7)

R <u>L</u> <u>P</u> A E

N <u>I</u> <u>L</u> E <u>N</u>

<u>D</u> <u>D</u> R <u>E</u> L <u>A</u>

B Y <u>M</u> <u>S</u> L <u>O</u>

Joshua led the Israelites to reach the . . .

_____ _____

(8)   (4)

H T <u>M</u> <u>N</u> O

<u>O</u> <u>N</u> E S <u>T</u>

G <u>A</u> W <u>N</u> O <u>S</u>

<u>Y</u> V T <u>A</u> <u>I</u> N

Abraham is the father of . . .

_____	_____
(4)	(7)

R L E A P

R O W S M

D G R A N O

R E T N I W

Joseph, the son of Jacob, was able to interpret dreams. He was known as . . .

_____ _____
(1)   (7)

B R O <u>L</u> <u>A</u>

<u>W</u> <u>O</u> P R E

E <u>S</u> <u>F</u> <u>T</u> R E

P P <u>L</u> A <u>A</u> E

The Ten Commandments were two . . .

_____	_____	_____
(5)	(2)	(4)

R E K B A

A L E S C

R I P C T S

L L A N O G

A place of worship was the . . .

(10)

L I E D F

O P D T A

I N R P G S

O O H C L S

David and Jonathan were . . .

_____   _____
(4)   (7)

L E P E S

H U M T B

B M E M L A

R H T N U E

Jesus was born in the city of . . .

———————
(9)

D <u>U</u> G E J

P <u>I</u> C <u>S</u> E

C K O S <u>T</u> <u>E</u>

A A R <u>C</u> L N

Amos and Dr. Martin Luther King, Jr. preached about . . .

(7)

SPOIL

STOOL

SHIELD

KIDNEY

It Holy

LIGHT

PLANT

PILLOW

GARDEN

I will go

FAITH

JUDGE

PRAISE

NUMBER

Hate a sin

ANGEL

ALONG

VIRGIN

SETTLE

All in love

ROBES

YEAST

REGION

DISCUS

Say no to drugs.

BIRTH

FALSE

DEEPLY

BURIAL

The bread

MONTH

PETRA

SANDAL

MOUSE

Moses

WHEAT

SATAN

MARTYR

VANITY

He ran away.

EARTH
NAVEL
DEATH
COLONY

A Deacon

SELAH

GROUND

INSECT

SINGLE

Sing a song

TABLE

YOUNG

RODENT

MASTER

A Martyr

PRIDE

OLIVE

LAWYER

PATMOS

My people

MEALS

CEDAR

CATTLE

MILDEW

A miracle

SHALL

GREEN

MAKETH

DEGREE

Leader

GHOST
HERON
FAMINE
FLEECE

A fisher of men.

BRICK

SNAIL

GADFLY

SPIDER

A king

MANNA

FLOCK

SWORD

QUIVER

Man of valor.

BROCK

ATONE

CYMBAL

SPRING

By stoning.

QUAIL
ADDED
EMBALM
ANOINT

Mind to build.

CHAIN

GRACE

GARDEN

CASTLE

Heart

ANGEL

NIGHT

SHRIVE

PLEDGE

A virgin

GNASH
NIGHT
COPPER
ARMORY

Synoptic

MERCY

BRASS

ONIONS

SPIRIT

Missionary

MOUTH

ANGER

MASTER

PARENT

Tongues

SOWER

POWER

HANDLE

WEALTH

"Reap what we sow."

FROST
FRUIT
ANOINT
GIANTS

Transfiguration

CROWN

SNORE

GARLIC

BUSHEL

Hung on a cross.

SHAVE

ONION

NATURE

CLOSET

Salvation

TENTS

PORCH

TONGUE

WEALTH

Pentateuch

SHRUB

LIGHT

BURDEN

WINTER

Burning bush

SOWER

SIEGE

ELEVEN

SPRING

Sovereign

WATCH

WEDGE

SCROLL

PARDON

Was the Word.

SPEAR ANGEL SCRIPT TRIALS

Parents

NIGHT

MANNA

SINGER

SPIRIT

In a manger

POWER

NIGHT

DEMONS

CASTLE

The prodigal son

POWER

PRESS

WEALTH

TEMPLE

Prophetess

SWINE
SWEAT
TRIALS
LEGION

Water into wine.

BOOTH

NIGHT

SHRINE

SISTER

Birthright

PLAIN

PRIDE

VESSEL

WILLOW

Wilderness

PLANT
TRIBE
ARCHER
ANIMAL

Parable

BROOK

WINGS

SHADOW

SURETY

Dry bones

FABLE

PRESS

DIADEM

BASKET

Blessed

PEARL

LINEN

LADDER

SYMBOL

Promised Land

MONTH

STONE

WAGONS

VANITY

Many Nations

PEARL
WORMS
DRAGON
WINTER

A Dreamer

LABOR

POWER

FOREST

APPEAL

Table of Laws

BAKER

SCALE

SCRIPT

GALLON

Tabernacle

FIELD

ADOPT

SPRING

SCHOOL

Good Friends

SLEEP

THUMB

EMBALM

HUNTER

Bethlehem

JUDGE

SPICE

SOCKET

CARNAL

Justice